AF207451

We believe in the power of design to influence
the way people work, learn, live and heal.

Welcome. Come inside.

  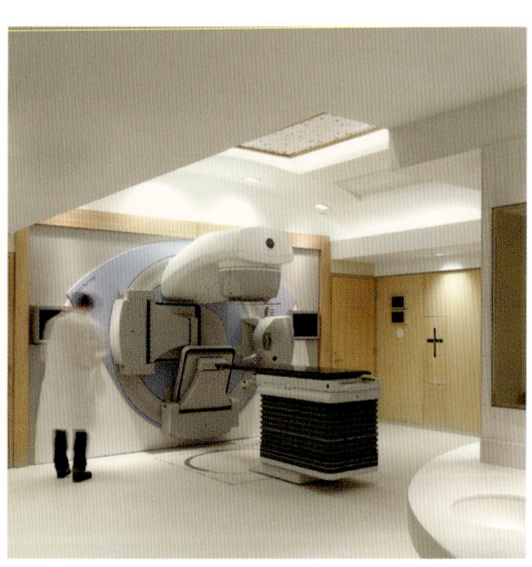

AVOID DEEP DIVES

CAUTION -   NO DIVING

JUST
The Sandbox

Antron
Antron
carpet fiber

GALVESTON NATIONAL LABORATORY: UNIVERSITY OF TEXAS MEDICAL BRANCH / GALVESTON, TX, USA

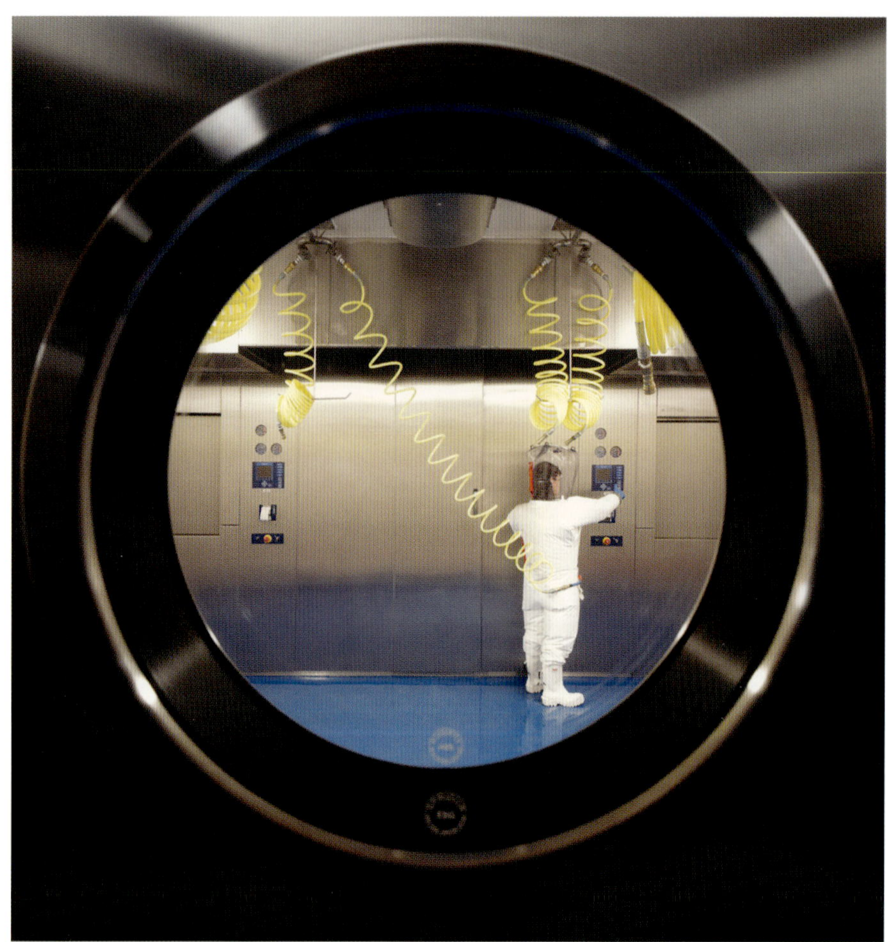

CHICAGO
VIENNA
WARSAW
PARIS
BRUSSELS

Breathe Deep

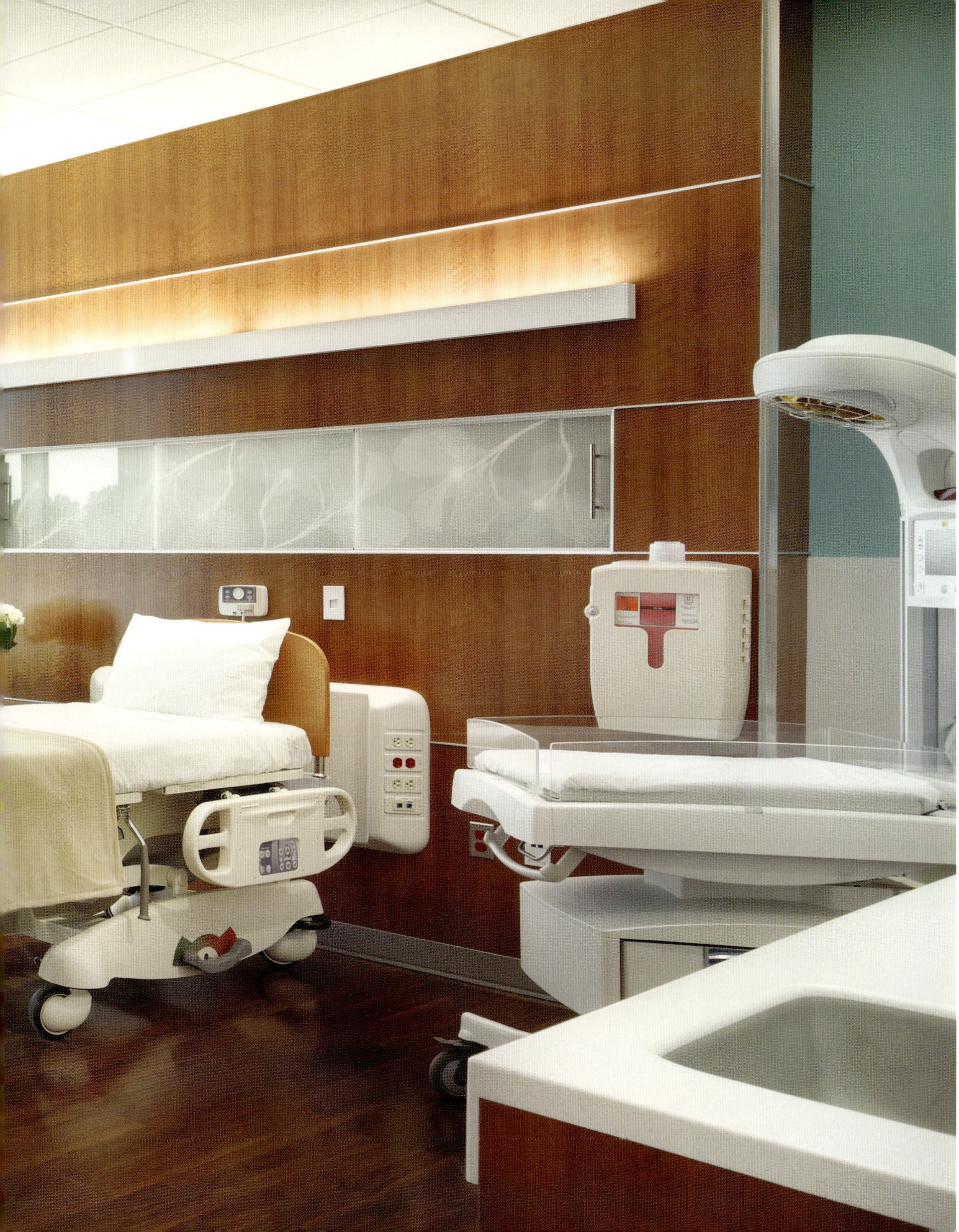

EINSTEIN MEDICAL CENTER MONTGOMERY / EAST NORRITON, PA, USA

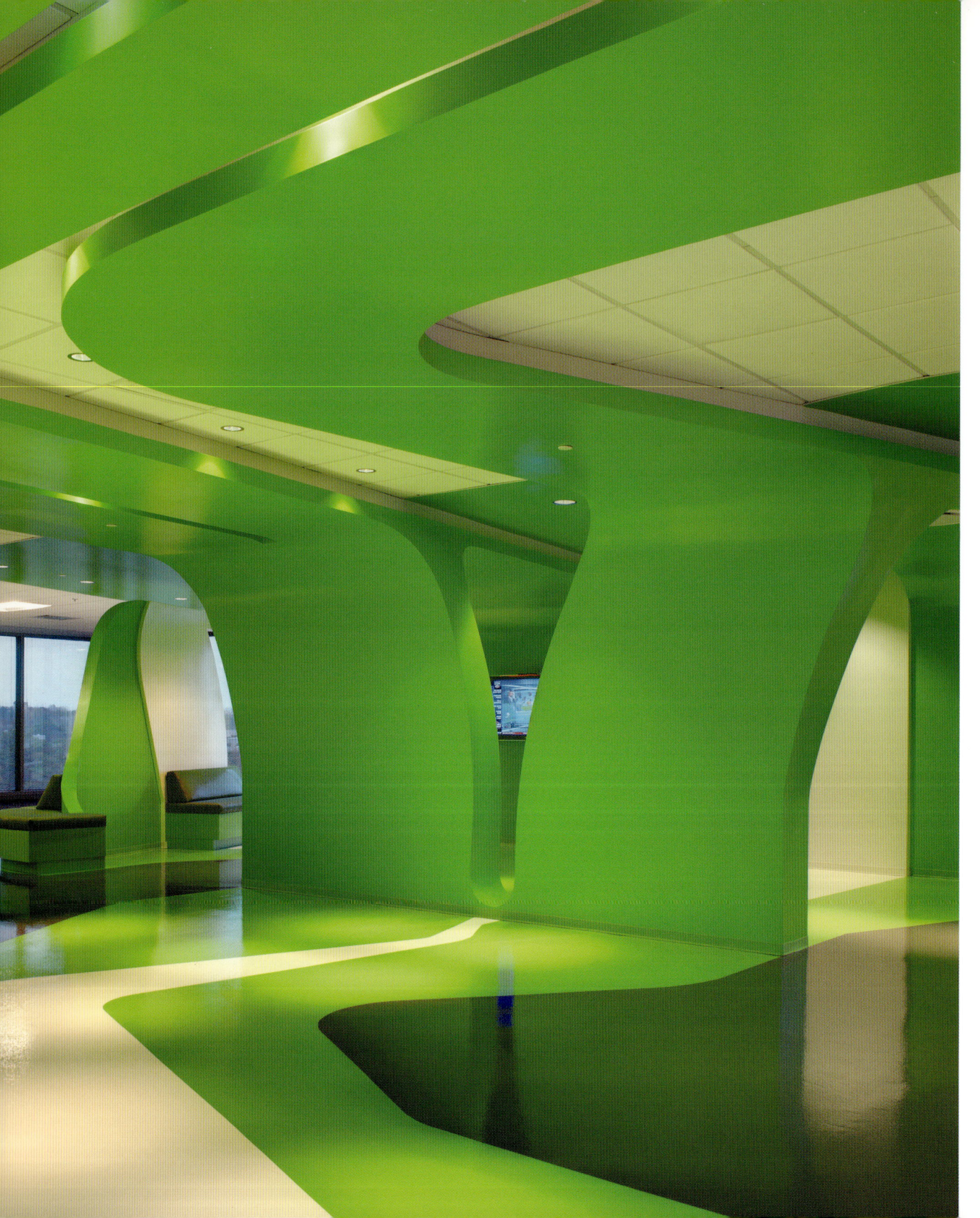

LEFTFIELD
DASANI

jump trading

MAIN CONCOURSE
SECTIONS 101-110
& MCARTHUR CLUBS
THE DUCK STORE
ELLOWS
KLAMATH

BE LEGENDARY
BE BOLD   BE DETERMINED   BE FOCUSED   BE HUMBLE
O

CompTIA

Redefining
What is Possible
cobalt

dynamic TEAMWORK
collaborate fresh
global
ENGAGE PASSION CHALLENGE
energy INSPIRE
CREATE
EXPLORE POSSIBILITY

ELEVATORS

RICHARD E. LINDNER CENTER, UNIVERSITY OF CINCINNATI / CINCINNATI, OH, USA

88

Washroom
Volunteer Lounge
Admissions

SCI MEDICAL
ONCOLOGY

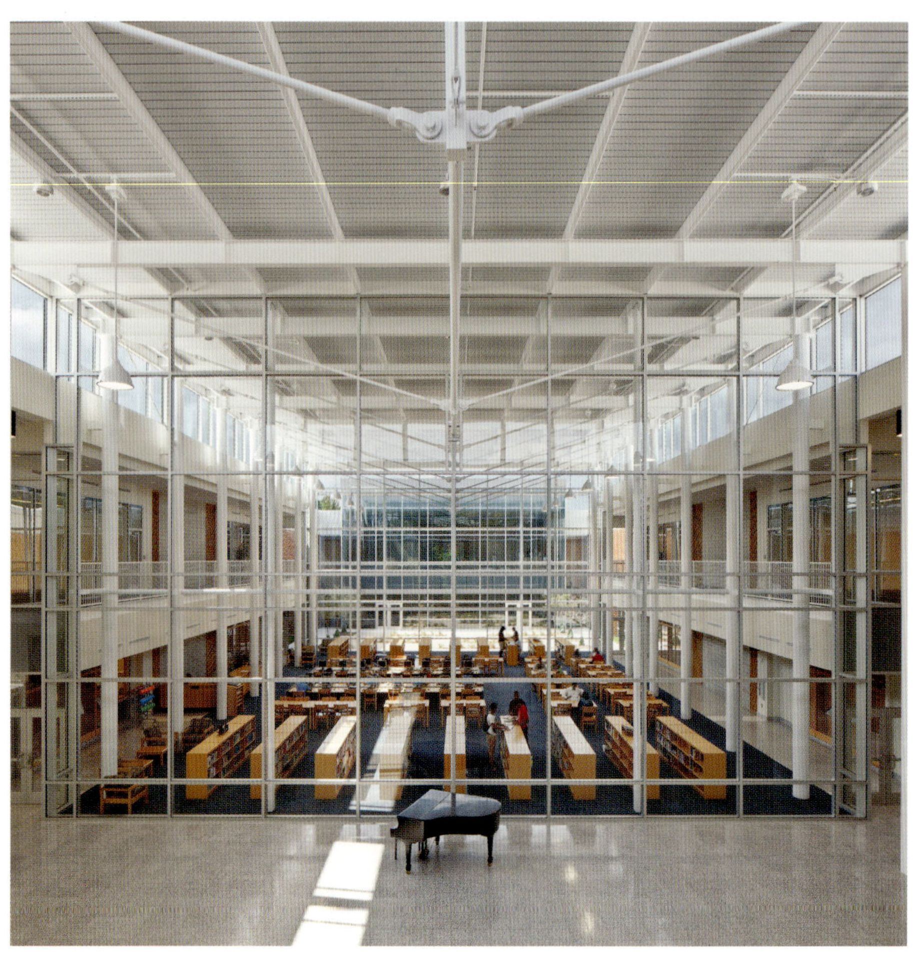

63 CONVENTION CENTER

118

ALLEN & OVERY / 28 - 29
London, UK, GBR
Project Size: 500,000 square feet
Project Team: Jack Pringle, Fiona Ballance,
Linzi Cassels, Peter Lill, Stephen Cork, Asha Genat
Photographer: David Churchill

ANTRON RESOURCE CENTER / 26 - 27
Chicago, IL, USA
Project Size: 3,000 square feet
Project Team: Eileen Jones, Keith Curtis, Kimberly
Richter, Brian Weatherford, Kay Lee, Katie Janson,
Cary Bohlen, Patrick Grzybek, Brian Erlinder, Liz
Mohl, Liz Potokar, Amanda McKenzie, Ron Stelmarski,
Melissa Kleve, Paul Hagle
Photographers: Colby Kidd / The Right Exposure (page
26), Steve Hall © Hedrich Blessing Photographers
(top row page 27), Eileen Jones (bottom left page 27),
Colby Kidd (bottom right, page 27)
Partner Firm: Float4 Interactive
Client: INVISTA

ASTELLAS / 44 - 45
London, UK, GBR
Project Size: 100,000 square feet
Project Team: Linzi Cassels, Charles Vine, Mariana
Dietrich, David Halpenny, Vicki Moffat, Siobhan O'Leary
Photographer: David Churchill

AUTOTRADER.COM / 56 - 57
Atlanta, GA, USA
Project Size: 400,000 square feet
Project Team: Joyce Fownes, Meena Krenek,
Christy Cain, Ping Wong
Photographer: © Nigel Marson Photography

BENJAMIN E. MAYS HIGH SCHOOL / 108 - 109
Atlanta, GA, USA
Project Size: 360,000 square feet
Project Team: Barbara Crum, Susanne Blam, Jack Allin,
Nazeer Kutty
Photographer: © Jonathan Hillyer
Client: Atlanta Public Schools

BRAINPOP / 84 - 85
New York, NY, USA
Project Size: 9,200 square feet
Project Team: Ken Wilson, David Kay, Michelle
LeTourneur, Lane Miller
Photographer: Eric Laignel

COMPTIA / 76 - 77
Downers Grove, IL, USA
Project Size: 35,000 square feet
Project Team: Gina Berndt, Eric Mersmann,
Jason Rosenblatt, Li-Pei Schweder, Melissa Kleve,
Roberto Ordonez
Photographer: Steve Hall © Hedrich Blessing
Photographers

CONFIDENTIAL INVESTMENT FIRM / 04 - 05
Chicago, IL, USA
Project Size: 24,000 square feet
Project Team: Thomas Kasznia, Michael Byun,
Daniel Biver, Amina Helstern, Melissa Kleve
Photographer: Steve Hall © Hedrich Blessing
Photographers

CONFIDENTIAL CLIENT / 124 - 125
Chicago, IL, USA
Project Size: 75,000 square feet
Project Team: Thomas Kasznia, Eric Mersmann,
Tim Wolfe, Sarah Kuchar, Ady Chu, Rocco Tunzi,
Andrew Wright
Photographer: © The Michelle Litvin Studio

CONFIDENTIAL BANKING CLIENT / 34 - 35
Charlotte, NC, USA
Project Size: 750,000 square feet
Project Team: Aki Knezevic, Eva Maddox, Ralph
Johnson, Tom Mozina, David Gieser, Jennifer Carzoli,
Kay Lee, Janice Barnes, Rod Vickroy, Mike Palmer,
Frank Pettinati, Joe Connell, Jeff Phillips, Ken Soch,
Robert Neper, Fred Schmidt, Simon Trude, Julie
Michiels, Daniel Figatner, Courtney Ruhl, Manchun
Chan, Chris Meuller, Elicia Gibbon, Michael Margulis,
Elise Rainville, Billy Simcox, Michelle Halle-Stern,
Anne Jackson, Greg Zirkle
Photographers: Steve Hall © Hedrich Blessing
Photographers (page 34), © James Steinkamp (page 35)

DUPLEX VILA MADALENA RESIDENCE / 10 - 11
São Paulo, SP, BRA
Project Size: 130 square meters
Project Team: Marcela Kishi, Gustavo Bergman,
Eloise Pucci, Nathalia Mouco, Ana Cecilia Guimarães,
Fernanda Borges
Photographer: Lufe Gomes
Client: Adriana Campello

**EINSTEIN MEDICAL CENTER
MONTGOMERY** / 42 - 43
East Norriton, PA, USA
Project Size: 360,000 square feet
Project Team: Rob Goodwin, Carolyn BaRoss,
Chris Bormann, Jean Mah, Bill Nation, Anthony Caputo,
Laura Morris, Danielle Masucci, Jennifer Tinsley,
John Rodenbeck, Rick Paul, Tim Nichols, Julio Colon,
Cheryl Woo, Robert Stansell, Odit Oliner, Ming Leung,
Sally Hinderegger, Brenda Byrd, Billy Simcox,
Steve Danielpour
Photographer: © Halkin/Mason Photography
Client: Einstein Healthcare Network

EMPORIO BAGLIONI RESTAURANT / 20 - 21
São Paulo, SP, BRA
Project Size: 550 square meters
Project Team: Douglas Tolaine, Giovana Oliva
Photographer: Daniel Ducci
Client Name: Luiz Eduardo Francez

**FAIRVIEW SOUTHDALE HOSPITAL MEDITATION
SPACE** / 66 - 67
Edina, MN, USA
Project Size: 1,500 square feet
Project Team: Sandy Christie, Linda Landry,
Lindsey Evenson, Michelle Hammer, Jerry Worrell
Photographer: Lucie Marusin

**GALVESTON NATIONAL LABORATORY: UNIVERSITY
OF TEXAS MEDICAL BRANCH** / 30
Galveston, TX, USA
Project Size: 194,000 square feet
Project Team: Ray Beets, Scott Sandlin, Jeff Kim,
Manuel Cadrecha, Dan Watch
Photographer: Nick Merrick © Hedrich Blessing
Photographers

SAMUEL BRIGHOUSE ELEMENTARY SCHOOL /
40 - 41
Richmond, BC, CAN
Project Size: 51,419 square feet
Project Team: Peter Busby, Robert Drew, Bob Greig,
Rod Maas, Penny Martyn, Teresa Miller, Joshua Rudd,
Adam Slawinski, Adriana Shum, Julie Verville,
Liam Woofter, James Kerrigan, Wendell Vaughn,
Christopher A. Waight, Crystal Wang
Photographers: Nic Lehoux (page 40), Latreille Delage
Photography (page 41)
Client: School District No: 38, Richmond, BC

SAN FRANCISCO CONSERVATORY
OF MUSIC / 36 - 37
San Francisco, CA, USA
Project Size: 126,000 square feet
Project Team: Cathy Simon, John Long
Photographer: Tim Griffith

SCHIFF HARDIN / 68 - 69
Washington, DC, USA
Project Size: 23,000 square feet
Project Team: Grzegorz Kosmal, Cassandra Cullison,
David Cordell, Marian Danowski, Haley Russell,
Kate Magee
Photographer: Prakash Patel

SWEDISH TRUE FAMILY WOMEN'S CANCER CENTER /
104 - 105
Seattle, WA, USA
Project Size: 28,000 square feet
Project Team: Brad Hinthorne, Erik Mott,
Mieke Stethem, Holly Herzer
Photographer: Juan Hernandez
Client: Swedish Medical Center

TEXTILE TRADING COMPANY / 114 - 115
São Paulo, SP, BRA
Project Size: 400 square meters
Project Team: Ilva Kanno, Giovanna Oliva,
Cesar Tadao, Nathalia Mouco, Daniela Cardoso
Photographer: Daniel Ducci
Client Name: Ozair P. Almeida

THOMAS JEFFERSON INDEPENDENT DAY
SCHOOL: FINE ARTS WING / 92 - 93
Joplin, MO, USA
Project Size: 53,000 square feet
Project Team: Steven Turckes, Jerry Johnson,
Christopher Hale, James Jeffs, Max Adams,
Aaron Manns, Hannah Jeffries, Eileen Jones,
Kelley Bozarth, Brian Erlinder, Liz Potokar,
Lynette Klein
Photographer: © Charles Davis Smith AIA
Associate Architect: Crafton Tull Sparks

UNILEVER / 118 - 119
London, UK, GBR
Project Size: 70,450 square feet
Project Team: Linzi Cassels, Francesca Gernone,
Annetta King
Photographer: Morley von Sternberg

UNIVERSITY OF THE ARTS / 70 - 71
London, UK, GBR
Project Size: 280,000 square feet
Project Team: William Poole-Wilson, Simon Bone,
Annette Diziol, Roshan Gunga, Jagath Panawala
Photographer: Rob Brown

UNIVERSITY OF NORTHWESTERN / 46 - 47
Saint Paul, MN, USA
Project Size: 61,000 square feet
Project Team: Trevor Dickie, Dave Dimond,
Mark Enlow, Jim Foran, Michelle Hammer,
Edward Heinen, Todd Lenthe, Paul Neuhaus,
Krisan Osterby, Larry Page, Melissa Rasmussen,
Dennis Sachs, Tim Vaughn, Jeff Ziebarth
Photographer: Paul Crosby

UNIVERSITY OF TORONTO: MISSISSAUGA
INSTRUCTIONAL CENTRE / 100 - 101
Mississauga, ON, CAN
Project Size: 155,000 square feet
Project Team: D'Arcy Arthurs, Andrew Frontini,
Alan Mortsch, Michelle Sta. Ana-Ascenzi
Photographer: Ben Rahn / A-Frame

UNIVERSITY OF WASHINGTON: SCHOOL OF
MEDICINE PHASE 2 / 31
Seattle, WA, USA
Project Size: 441,640 square feet
Project Team: Anthony Gianopoulos, Andrew Clinch,
Kelly Schnell, Sara Robinson
Photographer: Benjamin Benschneider

UNIVERSITY OF WATERLOO: ENGINEERING 5
BUILDING / 24 - 25
Waterloo, ON, CAN
Project Size: 154,000 square feet
Project Team: Werner Sommer, Andrew Frontini,
Liz Livingston
Photographer: Lisa Logan
Partner Firm: Somfay Marsi Architects

USGBC HEADQUARTERS / 08 - 09
Washington, DC, USA
Project Size: 75,000 square feet
Project Team: Ken Wilson, Rod Letonja, Summer
Minchew, Katie Lombardi, Sean Dorsy, Daniel Norman,
Ashley Compton
Photographer: Eric Laignel

VANDUSEN BOTANICAL GARDEN VISITOR CENTRE /
98 - 99
Vancouver, BC, CAN
Project Size: 19,000 square feet
Project Team: Chessa Adsit-Morris, Peter Busby,
Aneta Chmiel, Paul Cowcher, Robert Drew, Ben Engle-
Folchert, Robin Glover, Harley Grusko, Jacqueline
Ho, Rebecca Holt, Jim Huffman, Ellen Lee, Matthew
Lemay, Penny Martyn, Joanna Peacock, Max Richter,
Soren Schou
Photographer: Nic Lehoux
Client: Vancouver Board of Parks and Recreation

ZUBI ADVERTISING / 22 - 23
Coral Gables, FL, USA
Project Size: 21,425 square feet
Project Team: Marlene Liriano, Yenny Calabrese,
Lilia Gonzalez, Amanda Villa
Photographer: Robin Hill Photography

To learn more about Perkins+Will, visit: www.perkinswill.com

Special thanks: Gina Berndt, Joan Blumenfeld, Loren Cavallin,
Grzegorz Kosmal, Marlene Liriano, Deidre Mick, Chika Sekiguchi.

Published by: ORO Editions
Publishers of Architecture, Art, and Design
Gordon Goff: Publisher
www.oroeditions.com
info@oroeditions.com

Copyright © 2013 by ORO Editions
ISBN: 978-1-941806-09-8
10 09 08 07 06 5 4 3 2 1 First Edition

Color Separations and Printing: ORO Group Ltd.
Printed in China.

All rights reserved. No part of this book may be reproduced, stored in a
retrieval system, or transmitted in any form or by any means, including
electronic, mechanical, photocopying of microfilming, recording, or
otherwise, without written permission from the publisher.

This book was printed and bound using a variety of sustainable manufacturing processes and materials including soy-based inks, aqueous-based varnish, VOC- and formaldehyde-free glues, and phthalate-free laminations. The text is printed using offset sheetfed lithographic printing process in four color on 157gsm premium matte art paper with an off-line gloss aqueous spot varnish applied to all photographs.

ORO Editions makes a continuous effort to minimize the overall carbon footprint of its publications. As part of this goal, ORO Editions, in association with Global ReLeaf, arranges to plant trees to replace those used in the manufacturing of the paper produced for its books. Global ReLeaf is an international campaign run by American Forests, one of the world's oldest nonprofit conservation organizations. Global ReLeaf is American Forests' education and action program that helps individuals, organizations, agencies, and corporations improve the local and global environment by planting and caring for trees.

Library of Congress data: Available upon request

For information on our distribution, please visit our website:
www.oroeditions.com

Great clients make great projects.